MW01609981

Table of Contents

Introduction

Psilocybin (4-phosphoryloxy-N,N-dimethyltryptamine) and psilocin are chemical compounds obtained from certain types of dried or fresh hallucinogenic mushrooms found in Mexico, South America and the southern and northwest regions of the United States. Psilocybin is classified as an indole-alkylamine (tryptamine). These compounds have similar structure to lysergic acid diethylamide (LSD), and are abused for their hallucinogenic and euphoric effects to produce a "trip". Hallucinogenic (psychedelic) effects are probably due to action on central nervous system serotonin (5-HT) receptors.

There are over 180 species of mushrooms that contain the chemicals psilocybin or psilocin. Like the peyote (mescaline), hallucinogenic mushrooms

3

have been used in native or religious rites for centuries. Both psilocybin and psilocin can also be produced synthetically in the lab. There have been reports that psilocybin bought on the streets can actually be other species of mushrooms laced with LSD.

What are Psilocybin Mushrooms?

Before we go into more details, what exactly are psilocybin mushrooms? Psilocybin mushrooms are the most popular "magic mushrooms", which means that they are mushrooms with psychoactive properties. They are considered sacred medicine among indigenous tribes, having been used extensively in the past in religious and spiritual ceremonies, especially in Central and South America.

Although currently they are classified as a Schedule 1 drugs in the United States (and many other countries), recent John Hopkins research seems very promising. Some studies have shown that consuming psilocybin mushrooms can have a beneficial effect for individuals suffering from various psychiatric disorders, from anxiety to OCD and depression.

Another study from Johns Hopkins University showed that most of the participants rated this as one of the most significant spiritual experiences of their lives. It also proved that ingesting psilocybin mushrooms creates long-lasting positive personality changes in the users.

History

Early

Prehistoric rock art near Villar del Humo, Spain, offers a hypothesis that Psilocybe hispanica was used in religious rituals 6,000 years ago,[4] and that art at the Tassili caves in southern Algeria from 7,000 to 9,000 years ago may show the species Psilocybe mairei.

Pre-Columbian mushroom stones

Hallucinogenic species of the Psilocybe genus have a history of use among the native peoples of Mesoamerica for religious communion, divination, and healing, from pre-Columbian times to the present day. Mushroom stones and motifs have been found in Guatemala. A statuette dating from ca. 200 CE. and depicting a mushroom strongly resembling Psilocybe mexicana was found in a west Mexican shaft and chamber tomb in the state of Colima. A Psilocybe species was known to the Aztecs as teōnanācatl (literally "divine mushroom" - agglutinative form of teōtl (god, sacred) and nanācatl (mushroom) in Náhuatl) and were reportedly served at the coronation of the Aztec ruler Moctezuma II in 1502. Aztecs and Mazatecs referred to psilocybin mushrooms as genius mushrooms, divinatory mushrooms, and wondrous mushrooms, when translated into English. Bernardino de Sahagún reported ritualistic use of teonanácatl by the Aztecs, when he traveled to Central America after the expedition of Hernán Cortés.

After the Spanish conquest, Catholic missionaries campaigned against the cultural tradition of the Aztecs, dismissing the Aztecs as idolaters, and the use of hallucinogenic plants and mushrooms, like other pre-Christian traditions, was quickly suppressed. The Spanish believed the mushroom allowed the Aztecs and others to communicate with devils. In converting people to Catholicism, the Spanish pushed for a switch from teonanácatl to the

Catholic sacrament of the Eucharist. Despite this history, in some remote areas, the use of teonanácatl has persisted.

The first mention of hallucinogenic mushrooms in European medicinal literature appeared in the London Medical and Physical Journal in 1799: a man had served Psilocybe semilanceata mushrooms that he had picked for breakfast in London's Green Park to his family. The doctor who treated them later described how the youngest child "was attacked with fits of immoderate laughter, nor could the threats of his father or mother refrain him."

European use

In 1955, Valentina Pavlovna Wasson and R. Gordon Wasson became the first known European Americans to actively participate in an indigenous mushroom ceremony. The Wassons did much to publicize their experience, even publishing an article on their experiences in Life in May 13, 1957. In 1956 Roger Heim identified the psychoactive mushroom that the Wassons had brought back from Mexico as Psilocybe, and in 1958, Albert Hofmann first identified psilocybin and psilocin as the active compounds in these mushrooms.

Inspired by the Wassons' Life article, Timothy Leary traveled to Mexico to experience psilocybin mushrooms firsthand. Upon returning to Harvard in

1960, he and Richard Alpert started the Harvard Psilocybin Project, promoting psychological and religious study of psilocybin and other psychedelic drugs. After Leary and Alpert were dismissed by Harvard in 1963, they turned their attention toward promoting the psychedelic experience to the nascent hippie counterculture.

The popularization of entheogens by Wasson, Leary, authors Terence McKenna and Robert Anton Wilson, and others has led to an explosion in the use of psilocybin mushrooms throughout the world. By the early 1970s, many psilocybin mushroom species were described from temperate North America,

Europe, and Asia and were widely collected. Books describing methods of cultivating Psilocybe cubensis in large quantities were also published. The availability of psilocybin mushrooms from wild and cultivated sources has made it among the most widely used of the psychedelic drugs.

At present, psilocybin mushroom use has been reported among some groups spanning from central Mexico to Oaxaca, including groups of Nahua, Mixtecs, Mixe, Mazatecs, Zapotecs, and others. An important figure of mushroom usage in Mexico was María Sabina, who used native mushrooms, such as Psilocybe mexicana in her practice.

Global distribution of 100+ psychoactive species of genus Psilocybe mushrooms.

Many of these are found in Mexico (53 species), with the remainder distributed in Canada and the US (22), Europe (16), Asia (15), Africa (4), and Australia and associated islands. In general, psilocybin-containing species are dark-spored, gilled mushrooms that grow in meadows and woods of the subtropics and tropics, usually in soils rich in humus and plant debris. Psilocybin mushrooms occur on all continents, but the majority of species are found in subtropical humid forests. Psilocybe species commonly found in the tropics include P. cubensis and P. subcubensis. P. semilanceata, considered the world's most widely distributed psilocybin mushroom, is found in Europe, North America, Asia, South America, Australia and New Zealand, although it is absent from Mexico.

Effects

Psilocin

This section needs more medical references for verification or relies too heavily on primary sources. Please review the contents of the section and add the appropriate references if you can. Unsourced or poorly sourced material may be challenged and removed.

Rod of Asclepius2.svg

The effects of psilocybin mushrooms come from psilocybin and psilocin. When psilocybin is ingested, it is broken down to produce psilocin, which is responsible for the psychedelic effects. Psilocybin and psilocin create short-term increases in tolerance of users, thus making it difficult to abuse them because the more often they are taken within a short period of time, the weaker the resultant effects are. Psilocybin mushrooms have not been known to cause physical or psychological dependence (addiction). The psychedelic effects tend to appear around 20 minutes after ingestion and will last approximately 6 hours. Physical effects including nausea, vomiting, euphoria, muscle weakness or relaxation, drowsiness, and lack of coordination may occur.

As with many psychedelic substances, the effects of psychedelic mushrooms are subjective and can vary considerably among individual users. The mind-altering effects of psilocybin-containing mushrooms typically last from three to eight hours depending on dosage, preparation method, and personal metabolism. The first 3–4 hours of the trip are typically referred to as the 'peak'—in which the user experiences more vivid visuals, and distortions in reality. However, the effects can seem to last much longer to the user because of psilocybin's ability to alter time perception.

Despite risks, mushrooms do much less damage in the UK than other recreational drugs.

Sensory

Sensory effects include visual and auditory hallucinations followed by emotional changes and altered perception of time and space. Noticeable changes to the auditory, visual, and tactile senses may become apparent around 30 minutes to an hour after ingestion, although effects may take up to two hours to take place. These shifts in perception visually include enhancement and contrasting of colors, strange light phenomena (such as auras or "halos" around light sources), increased visual acuity, surfaces that seem to ripple, shimmer, or breathe; complex open and closed eye visuals of form constants or images, objects that warp, morph, or change solid colours; a sense of melting into the environment, and trails behind moving objects. Sounds may seem to have increased clarity—music, for example, can take on a profound sense of cadence and depth. Some users experience synesthesia, wherein they perceive, for example, a visualization of color upon hearing a particular sound.

Emotional

As with other psychedelics such as LSD, the experience, or 'trip', is strongly dependent upon set and setting. Hilarity, depression, lack of concentration, and muscular relaxation (including dilated pupils) are all normal effects, sometimes in the same trip. A negative environment could contribute to a bad trip, whereas a comfortable and familiar environment would set the stage for a pleasant experience. Psychedelics make experiences more intense, so if a person enters a trip in an anxious state of mind, they will likely experience heightened anxiety on their trip. Many users find it preferable to ingest the mushrooms with friends or people who are familiar with 'tripping'. The psychological consequences of psilocybin use include hallucinations and an inability to discern fantasy from reality. Panic reactions and psychosis also may occur, particularly if a user ingests a large dose. In addition to the risks associated with ingestion of psilocybin, individuals who seek to use psilocybin mushrooms also risk poisoning if one of the many varieties of poisonous mushrooms is confused with a psilocybin mushroom.

A study at Johns Hopkins University found that a dose of 20 to 30 mg psilocybin per 70 kg occasioning mystical-type experiences brought lasting positive changes to traits including altruism, gratitude, forgiveness and feeling close to others when it was combined with meditation and an extensive spiritual practice support programme. There is scientific evidence for a context- and state-dependent causal effect of psychedelic use on connection with nature.

How To Safely Identify Psilocybin Mushrooms

Have you ever heard of people ending up in the ER due to mushroom poisoning?

These frequent accidents occur due to the fact that people think they "know" which mushrooms are safe to eat and which are not. Reality shows us that many of t hem are wrong.

Things get even more complicated when it comes to psychoactive mushrooms (also called "magic mushrooms") due to the fact that the psychological profile of the persons willing to try this type of mushrooms includes a higher tolerance for risk.

That is why it is crucial to invest a lot of time in getting to know the specific characteristics of psilocybin mushrooms before you head out to pick them up and eat them. This can make the difference between having a pleasant spiritual experience of ending up in the ER with serious poisoning.

Here are a few important pointers on how to differentiate between psilocybin mushrooms. Make sure you extensively study pictures of these mushrooms and notice the differences between them.

Psilocybe semilanceata

These mushrooms are also known as "Liberty Caps" due to their large caps. They are known to be among the most potent psilocybin mushrooms. They also grow frequently in North America and throughout Europe

These mushrooms usually grow in meadows and pastures, often in those grazed by sheep. However, unlike psilocybe cubensis, psilocybe semilanceata do not grow directly out of dung.

Psilocybe mexicana

These mushrooms grow especially in Central and South America, where they have been used ceremonially for millennia. They are also called "teonanacatl". Similar in aspect to psilocybe semilanceata, it is hard to distinguish them from the latter.

Psilocybe cyanescens

This specific type of psilocybin mushrooms are also known as "Wavy Caps".

According to Jacob Akin from the University of Wisconsin, there seems to be evidence of this type of mushrooms at the ancient Egyptian hieroglyphs. Research is showing that these mushrooms were used by the ancient Egyptians for their psychoactive properties during religious ceremonies.

These mushrooms are also found in many areas throughout the world and are known to be quite potent when it comes to their psychedelic effects.

Psilocybe azurescens

This type of mushroom is also known as the "Flying Saucer Mushroom". It is also known as the most potent psychoactive psilocybin mushrooms due to the fact that it has the highest concentration of the psychoactive biochemicals, psilocybin and psilocin.

It often grows along the northern Oregon Coast, favoring the beachland interface. Psilocybe azurescens prefers to grow in dune grasses. It also causes the whitening of wood. Fruitings begin in late September and continue even after the first frost occurs, until late December or even January. It is a very adaptive species.

Psilocybe baeocystis

This type of mushroom is also known as "Knobby Tops". It is usually found on decaying conifer mulch, in wood chips, or in lawns with high lignin content.

It can also occasionally grow from fallen seed cones of Douglas fir.You can normally find these mushrooms in fall, even ranging to early winter but rarely in the spring.

Psilocybe cubensis

This is the most popular species of psilocybin mushrooms, also known as "Golden Teacher".

You may find it throughout southeastern United States, Central America and northern South America. It also grows throughout southeast Asia, in countries such as Thailand, India, Cambodia and Vietnam.

Normally, these mushrooms grow at their maximum size in the two months prior to the hottest period in the year. In the United States, this means you can find them in May and June most frequently, although they can also be found up until January.

Exercise Great Caution When Dealing With Psilocybin Mushrooms

Please exercise maximum caution when it comes to cultivating or growing psilocybin mushrooms. There is a very real risk of poisoning and even death. It is best to spend as much time as possible in studying extensively the characteristics of these magic mushrooms if you are serious about identifying and consuming them.

A great book on the subject is Paul Stamets' reference book on identifying psilocybin mushrooms around various parts of the world.

Make sure you also identify the visual differences between the mushrooms and become quite proficient at it before ingesting any type of psilocybin mushrooms.

Methods of Psilocybin Use

"Magic Mushrooms" have long, slender stems which may appear white or greyish topped by caps with dark gills on the underside. Dried mushrooms are usually a reddish rust brown color with isolated areas of off-white. Mushrooms are ingested orally and may be made into a tea or mixed into other foods. The mushrooms may be used as fresh or dried product. Psilocybin has a bitter, unpalatable taste.

A "bad trip", or a unpleasant or even terrifying experience, may occur with any dose of psilocybin.

In general, dried mushrooms contain about 0.2% to 0.4% psilocybin and only trace amounts of psilocin. The typical dose of psilocybin used for recreational purposes varies, with peak effects occurring in 1 to 2 hours, and lasting for about six hours.

Dose and effects can vary considerably depending upon mushroom type, method of preparation, and tolerance of the individual. It can be difficult to determine the exact species of mushroom or how much hallucinogen each mushroom contains. Initial smaller doses and a longer period of time to determine the effects may be a safer option if you choose to use psilocybin for recreational purposes.

Effects of 'Magic Mushroom' Use

Psilocybin effects are similar to those of other hallucinogens, such as mescaline from peyote or LSD. The psychological reaction to psilocybin use include visual and auditory hallucinations and an inability to discern fantasy from reality. Panic reactions and psychosis also may occur, particularly if large doses of psilocybin are ingested.

Hallucinogens that interfere with the action of the brain chemical serotonin may alter:

Mood

Sensory perception

Sleep

Hunger

Body temperature

Sexual behavior

Muscle control

Physical effects of psychedelic mushrooms may include a feeling of nausea, vomiting, muscle weakness, confusion, and a lack of coordination. Combined use with other substances, such as alcohol and marijuana can heighten, or worsen all of these effects.

Other effects of hallucinogenic drugs can include:

Intensified feelings and sensory experiences

Changes in sense of time (for example, time passing by slowly)

Increased blood pressure, breathing rate, or body temperature

Loss of appetite

Dry mouth

Sleep problems

Mixed senses (such as "seeing" sounds or "hearing" colors)

Spiritual experiences

Feelings of relaxation or detachment from self/environment

Uncoordinated movements

Lowered inhibition

Excessive sweating

Panic

Paranoia - extreme and unreasonable distrust of others

Psychosis - disordered thinking detached from reality

Larger psilocybin doses, including an overdose, can lead to intense hallucinogenic effects over a longer period of time. An intense "trip" episode may occur, which may involve panic, paranoia, psychosis, frightful visualizations ("bad trip"), and very rarely death. Memory of a "bad trip" can last a lifetime.

Abuse of psilocybin mushrooms could also lead to toxicity or death if a poisonous mushroom is incorrectly thought to be a "magic" mushroom and ingested. If vomiting, diarrhea, or stomach cramps begin several hours after consuming the mushrooms, the possibility of poisoning with toxic mushrooms should be considered, and emergency medical care should be sought immediately.

Tolerance to the use of psilocybin has been reported, which means a person needs an increasing larger dose to get the same hallucinogenic effect. "Flashbacks", similar to those occur in some people after using LSD, have also been reported with mushrooms. It is reported that people who use LSD or mescaline can build a cross-tolerance to psilocybin, as well.

How Long Do Mushrooms Stay in Your System?

Common hallucinogens, with the possible exception of phencyclidine (PCP), are not usually tested for on standard workplace drug screens. However, if desired by legal authorities, medical personnel, or an employer, it is possible to perform laboratory assays that can detect any drug or metabolite, including psilocybin, via advanced techniques.

When tested via urine, the psilocybin mushroom metabolite psilocin can stay in your system for up to 3 days. However, metabolic rate, age, weight, age, medical conditions, drug tolerance, other drugs or medications used, and urine pH of each individual may affect actual detection periods.

Extent of Hallucinogenic Mushroom Use

Based on a 2018 survey from SAMHSA's National Survey on Drug Use and Health (NSDUH), about 5.6 million people aged 12 or older reported using hallucinogens (which may include psilocybin mushrooms) in the year prior to the survey. In 2017, that number was roughly 5.1 million. In the survey, hallucinogens include not only psilocybin from mushrooms, but also other psychedelic drugs like LSD, MDMA (Ecstasy, Molly), and peyote (mescaline). In comparison, 43.5 million people used marijuana in the year prior to the 2018 survey.

In 2018, there were 1.1 million people aged 12 and older who had used hallucinogens for the first time within the past year. In particular, college students, and people ages 18 to 25, may choose mushrooms as a drug of abuse.

Are Mushrooms Legal in the U.S.?

Psilocybin is a Schedule I substance under the DEA's Controlled Substances Act, which means that it has a high potential for abuse, no currently accepted medical use in treatment in the U.S., and a lack of accepted safety for use under medical supervision. There are no commercial uses for psilocybin.

Currently, psilocybin is not available to doctors in the clinical setting because it is listed as a Schedule I drug by the US Drug Enforcement Agency (DEA). Researchers may only be able to get access to the illegal compound for the study through special waivers from the U.S. Food and Drug Administration (FDA). Other drugs found in Schedule I include marijuana, LSD, and heroin. In order for psilocybin to be prescribed for patients, it would have to be reclassified as a Schedule II medication, meaning it has a currently accepted medical use, but with severe restrictions due to addiction potential.

Medical Uses and Clinical Studies for Psilocybin

Although psilocybin has been used for centuries in rituals, modern medicine has recently reported clinical studies, as well. A report was published in the Journal of Psychopharmacology detailing two small studies that noted the ingredient in "magic mushrooms" - psilocybin - can reverse the feeling of "existential distress" that patients often feel after being treated for cancer. Reportedly, cancer can leave patients with this type of psychiatric disorder, feeling that life has no meaning. Typical treatments such as antidepressants may not be effective. However, use of a single dose of synthetic psilocybin reversed the distress felt by the patients and was a long-term effect. Some advanced cancer patients described the effect from the drug as if "the cloud of doom seemed to lift."

Two additional studies using psilocybin were completed: one at New York University (NYU) Langone Medical Center in New York City and one at Johns Hopkins Medical School in Baltimore. For both studies, trained monitors were with patients as they experienced the effects of the drug, which can lead to hallucinations.

In the NYU study, 29 patients with advanced cancer were given either a single dose of psilocybin or the B vitamin known as niacin, both in conjunction with psychotherapy. After seven weeks, the patients switched treatments (a cross-over study). In 60% to 80% of the patients receiving psilocybin, a relief from distress occurred rapidly and lasted over six months. The long-term effect was evaluated by researchers looking at test scores for depression and anxiety.

In the Johns Hopkins study, researchers treated 51 adults with advanced cancer with a small dose of psilocybin followed five weeks later with a higher dose, with a 6-month follow-up. As with the NYU study, about 80% of participants experienced clinically significant relief from their anxiety and depression that lasted up to six months.

At the Center for Psychedelic and Consciousness Research at Johns Hopkins University in Baltimore, Maryland, researchers are focusing on how psychedelics affect behavior, mood, cognition, brain function, and biological markers of health. This research group was the first to obtain U.S. regulatory approval to continue research with psychedelics in healthy volunteers.

Additional studies with psilocybin are expected, and one is comparing the chemical against a leading traditional antidepressant.

As reported by Johns Hopkins, upcoming studies will evaluate the use of psilocybin as a new therapy for opioid addiction, Alzheimer's disease, post-traumatic stress disorder (PTSD), post-treatment Lyme disease syndrome (formerly known as chronic Lyme disease), anorexia nervosa and alcohol use in people with major depression. A focus on precision medicine tailored to the individual patient is expected.

In November 2019, the FDA designated psilocybin therapy as a "breakthrough therapy" for depression to the Usona Institute, an action the agency uses to speed up development and review of investigational drugs. Breakthrough therapies are expected to provide a major improvement over currently available agents for an unmet medical need.

Usona's PSIL201 psilocybin U.S. clinical trial is a Phase 2 study evaluating psilocybin as a treatment for Major Depressive Disorder (MDD). This research will use a randomized, double-blind, placebo-controlled study design to measure the antidepressant effects of a single dose of psilocybin in 80 patients between 21 to 65 years of age with MDD. According to the manufacturer, "psilocybin potentially offers a novel paradigm in which a short-acting compound imparts profound alterations in consciousness and could enable long-term remission of depressive symptoms."

If FDA-approved, psilocybin would have to be reclassified by the DEA for it to be available for patients; it is currently classified as a Schedule I drug.

How to Identify Wild Mushrooms

Wild psilocybin mushrooms are found in many locations across the globe and occur in at least 10 different varieties. Some psilocybin-containing mushrooms have not been named as a strain yet and are simply called "unidentified." The most common of the wild psilocybin-containing mushrooms, Psilocybe cubensis, is found in the United States, Mexico, Central and South America and the West Indies. Psilocybin mushrooms can often be recognized by their color, shape and stem bruising, which produces a blue color. Psilocybin mushrooms should be carefully avoided because they carry major health risks and are illegal to use in the United States. The ingestion of these mushrooms can cause hallucinations, nausea, vomiting, drowsiness or even renal failure. Always carefully identify any mushroom in question before consumption to ensure that it is not of this type.

Wild brown mushrooms growing

Look at the color of the mushroom. Young Psilocybe cubensis mushrooms (typically these will be smaller ones) may be a deep golden brown color, while more mature ones are a lighter golden brown color.

Brown mushrooms growing

Look for a center marking. The Psilocybe cubensis has a distinct darker brown spot in the center of the mushroom.

Closeup view of a mushroom stem

Look at the stem of the mushroom to see if there is a blue hue. This color, which may be caused by an oxygen and psilocybin interaction, occurs with bruising of any type. If the mushroom has been touched by a human, insect, or even grass or other mushrooms this reaction is likely to occur.

Closeup of a mushroom's gills

Look for a deep purple colored gill cover. This mushroom veil is a very thin covering that stays on the mushroom gills until the mushroom cap fully expands, at which point it will break. A broken veil can often be observed circling the stems of psilocybin mushrooms.

Legal status of psilocybin mushrooms

For the legal status of the psychoactive substance found in psilocybin mushrooms, see psilocybin § Legal status, and psilocin § Legal status.

The legal status of unauthorised actions with psilocybin mushrooms varies worldwide. Psilocybin and psilocin are listed as Schedule I drugs under the United Nations 1971 Convention on Psychotropic Substances. Schedule I drugs are defined as drugs with a high potential for abuse or drugs that have no recognized medical uses. However, psilocybin mushrooms have had numerous medicinal and religious uses in dozens of cultures throughout history and have a significantly lower potential for abuse than other Schedule I drugs.

Psilocybin mushrooms are not regulated by UN treaties. From a letter, dated 13 September 2001, from Herbert Schaepe, Secretary of the UN International Narcotics Control Board, to the Dutch Ministry of Health:

As you are aware, mushrooms containing the above substances are collected and used for their hallucinogenic effects. As a matter of international law, no plants (natural material) containing psilocine and psilocybin are at present controlled under the Convention on Psychotropic Substances of 1971. Consequently, preparations made of these plants are not under international control and, therefore, not subject of the articles of the 1971 Convention [emphasis added]. Criminal cases are decided with reference to domestic law, which may otherwise provide for controls over mushrooms containing psilocine and psilocybin. As the Board can only speak as to the contours of the international drug conventions, I am unable to provide an opinion on the litigation in question.

Many countries, however, have some level of regulation or prohibition of psilocybin mushrooms (for example, the US Psychotropic Substances Act, the UK Misuse of Drugs Act 1971, and the Canadian Controlled Drugs and Substances Act). The prohibition of psilocybin mushrooms has come under criticism, from the general public and from researchers who see therapeutic potential with regard to drug addictions and other mental instabilities, such as PTSD, anxiety and depression, as well as cluster headaches. Among regulated drugs, psilocybin mushrooms also have relatively few medical risks.

In many national, state, and provincial drug laws, there is a great deal of ambiguity about the legal status of psilocybin mushrooms, as well as a strong element of selective enforcement in some places, since psilocybin and psilocin are deemed illegal to possess without license as substances, but mushrooms themselves are not mentioned in these laws. The legal status of Psilocybe spores is even more ambiguous, as the spores contain neither psilocybin nor psilocin, and hence are not illegal to sell or possess in many jurisdictions, though many jurisdictions will prosecute under broader laws prohibiting items that are used in drug manufacture. A few jurisdictions (such as the US states of Georgia and Idaho) have specifically prohibited the sale and possession of psilocybin mushroom spores. Cultivation of psilocybin mushrooms is considered drug manufacture in most jurisdictions and is often severely penalized, though some countries and one US state has ruled that growing psilocybin mushrooms does not qualify as "manufacturing" a controlled substance.

WHAT IS PSILOCYBIN MUSHROOM MICRODOSING?

Microdosing is the act of consuming sub-perceptual – unnoticeable – amounts of a psychedelic substance. Many individuals who have integrated microdosing psilocybin mushrooms into their weekly routine report higher levels of creativity, more energy, increased focus, and improved relational skills.

Some enthusiasts also report that microdosing psilocybin helps to heighten spiritual awareness and enhance their senses.

Eminent psychedelic researchers have also found largely positive effects of psilocybin mushrooms on mood disorders and anxiety.

In fact, The Beckley Foundation is spearheading the push for the legalization of psilocybin mushrooms, backed by long-term positive effects found in their research conducted on treatment-resistant depression patients. Recently, Oakland, California decriminalized all plant medicines including psilocybin mushrooms, a move that followed Denver Colorado's successful referendum to decriminalize psilocybin mushrooms.

Even addictions, such as smoking, can be overcome with psilocybin. Researchers at Johns Hopkins reported an 80 percent abstinence rate among a group of longtime smokers who took psilocybin as part of their cognitive behavioral therapy.

Aside from psychological issues, mushrooms (and LSD) have been found to be "comparable to or more efficacious than most conventional medications" in treating cluster headaches. Many people have experienced extended periods of remission after taking them.

With all these encouraging results reported from full doses, there's reason to believe that microdosing psilocybin could bring about similarly positive life changes.

THE HISTORY OF MICRODOSING

While the modern history of psychedelics reaches back to the 1950s, interest in microdosing saw a major revitalization with the publishing of Dr. James Fadiman's The Psychedelic Explorer's Guide: Safe, Therapeutic, and Sacred Journeys in 2011.

The book explores microdosing as a subculture of psychedelic use. While a number of indigenous cultures, as well as modern professionals, have used microdosing to unlock a host of benefits, Fadiman's book formally introduced the term "microdosing" into the psychedelic mainstream.

But the book didn't just contribute a piece of terminology; it awakened the curiosity and imaginations of millions of people. It also provided practical information for anyone who wanted to give it a try, much of which has been integrated into this guide.

Fadiman's ongoing research serves as one of the few modern studies into the effects of microdosing specifically (most other research deals with larger doses for specific therapeutic outcomes).

Following the publication of The Psychedelic Explorer's Guide, the next boost in the public's awareness of microdosing came from a podcast interview the author gave with Tim Ferriss in March of 2015.

Ferriss, who rose to fame after authoring the bestseller, the 4-Hour Work Week, has an enormous audience of individuals interested in entrepreneurship, "biohacking," self-experimentation, psychology, spirituality, and other subjects that predispose them to an interest in the benefits of microdosing.

His podcast interview with Fadiman blasted the core messages about microdosing contained in The Psychedelic Explorer's Guide from a soapbox loud enough to increase awareness of the practice.

Soon after its air date, listeners of Ferriss' podcast were not only starting to experiment with microdosing; they were discussing it with their own personal networks. Consequently, journalists began writing articles about microdosing, leading to even greater awareness and interest.

Another source of interest in microdosing came from Ayelet Waldman's 2016 book A Really Good Day: How Microdosing Made a Mega Difference in my Mood, My Marriage, and My Life.

Waldman's book discusses her 30-day protocol of microdosing with LSD to address a variety of psychological symptoms primarily caused by hormonal changes related to menopause.

Prior to microdosing, Waldman's mood swings had become severe enough to put her marriage and relationship with her children at risk.

Afterward, in an interview with The Third Wave, she said, "This month changed my life, and I am sad every day that I can't keep doing it legally."

Now, tens of thousands of people around the globe are being turned on to microdosing – whether it's for treating mental health problems, boosting creativity, or giving entrepreneurs new directions.

THE SCIENCE OF MICRODOSING PSILOCYBIN MUSHROOMS

While psychedelic substances have been illegal and prohibited from study in most countries up until the past few years, many leading experts have picked up on research that started in the 1950s and 60s.

While there has been some recent research on microdosing, we know more about what large doses of psychedelics do to the brain.

Much of what we understand about how psychedelics work involves serotonin, a chemical that is among the brain's most important neurotransmitters. Serotonin affects nearly everything we do, from how we feel to how we process information. It keeps our brains ticking.

Classic psychedelics such as LSD and psilocybin share a similar structure to serotonin, and work along a similar pathway. This is why these substances will have comparable effects when microdosed, too – at least in the most important aspects described in the Benefits and Risks section

59

of this guide. You can read more here about the differences between them.

Many antidepressants (called Selective Serotonin Reuptake Inhibitors, or SSRIs) try to make serotonin more plentiful in the brain to make you feel better.

Psychedelics work more directly, by mimicking serotonin. This means that one of their main effects is to stimulate a serotonin receptor called "5-HT2A" located in the prefrontal cortex.

Stimulating the 5-HT2A receptor leads to two important results:

The production of "Brain Derived Neurotrophic Factor" (BDNF) which is "like Miracle-Gro for your brain. It stimulates growth, connections, and activity."

The increased transmission of "Glutamate," the neurotransmitter most responsible for brain functions like cognition, learning, and memory.

Glutamate and BDNF work together in ways we're still understanding, but it's become clear that having more of each leads to many of the benefits that microdosers are seeking.

Psychedelics also cause parts of the brain that don't usually communicate with one another... to communicate with one another! These unique connections are formed by dampening the activity of an often over-used part of our brain called the "Default Mode Network" (DMN).

The DMN is responsible for an array of different mental activities, including day-dreaming, self-reflection, and thinking about the past or the future. Some studies suggest that depression is linked to an overactive DMN. Its possible that a highly active DMN causes us to ruminate, over-analyze ourselves, and constantly step out of the present moment to question the past and the future.

This helps explain why these substances could be used to combat depression and anxiety, and also lead to insights and creative perspectives that otherwise remain inaccessible to us.

FLOW STATES

All of us, at some point in our lives, have experienced a flow state. The surfer effortlessly riding a big wave, the therapist perfectly in-sync with her client, the salesman elegantly working the room...

Simply put, flow is one of the great experiences of being human.

We have no specific, non-anecdotal evidence to suggest that microdoses of psychedelics can induce flow states – but studies have shown moderate doses cause brain waves to shift toward alpha oscillations, which is also seen in the transition to a flow state.

Psychedelics such as psilocybin imitate the neurotransmitter serotonin when they enter the brain – and we know that serotonin is found in higher levels in flow states. Unlike LSD, however, psilocybin/psilocin appears to interact minimally and only indirectly with dopamine – another neurotransmitter associated with flow states. This interaction may be minimal in the microdose range.

Perhaps most important, psychedelics' ability to attenuate the DMN can allow our brains to make unique connections between areas that don't usually communicate. [4] This is crucial for allowing flow states to occur.

Since we know that moderate doses of psychedelics can induce similar effects to a flow state in the brain, it seems likely that a regular microdosing regimen could begin to shift our awareness in the direction of flow.

HOW DO YOU MICRODOSE WITH PSILOCYBIN MUSHROOMS?

Ideally, a psilocybin microdose will not cause a substantial change in mood, disposition, or mindset. Instead, its effect will be subtle but present.

Preparing psilocybin mushrooms for microdosing involves more steps than microdosing with LSD, but is still straightforward.

Not only will fresh and dried psilocybin mushrooms contain different quantities of psilocybin, but different strains of mushrooms will have different psilocybin contents. Even different parts of the mushroom contain slightly different amounts of psilocybin!

We recommend drying a batch of mushrooms, grinding them into a powder, and measuring out around 0.1g of powder as your starter microdose. You can then adjust the amount accordingly after your first attempt. When you take an amount that makes you feel some changes (most notably drowsiness, the first effect that comes on in a psilocybin trip), roll back to the dose just under it, and you will have found your mushroom microdose sweet spot.

You can use any kind of psilocybin mushrooms for your microdosing. The most popular ones are Psilocybe cubensis, Psilocybe semilanceata, Psilocybe azurecens, Psilocybe cyanescens, and Panaeolus. Just be aware how much psilocybin content your strain has (for example, the last two are rich in psilocybin), and adjust your microdose accordingly. You can learn about the potency levels of different Psilocybe strains at Erowid.

There are several ways to take your mushroom microdose. The most practical one is to measure out your dosages precisely, and fill up some empty capsules with the powder. This will ensure even distribution throughout your regimen, and will mitigate the taste issue that some people have with psilocybin mushrooms.

Another way is to prepare a psilocybin tea. You can dissolve your desired dose of mushroom powder in hot water, and even add some honey. Otherwise, you are free to experiment and mix the powder into any drink you take to start your day.

WHAT SCHEDULE SHOULD I FOLLOW?

James Fadiman recommends taking a microdose once every three days. For most people, morning is the best time because the beneficial effects will last throughout the day, and also because nighttime microdosing could interfere with sleep.

Take a mushroom microdose on Day 1. Then do not take a microdose on Day 2 or Day 3.

Then, take another mushroom microdose on Day 4.

Observe the effects throughout this process by taking daily notes in a journal.

Continue the process of microdosing two times per week for several weeks. Take notes throughout the entire process on both short-term, in-the-moment effects, and long-term changes in your mood, energy, and social behavior.

Follow your usual routine while microdosing. You should not change what you do. The purpose is to enhance your day-to-day existence by integrating microdoses into your routine.

However, when you try microdosing for the first time, take a day off from work and social commitments. It will give you a chance to observe and notice any unusual effects before microdosing in a more public situation.

Be vigilant in observing the effects of microdosing on the two days between doses. Many people perceive increased feelings of flow, creativity, and energy the day after they microdose, as well as the day of microdosing.

Microdosing every day is not recommended. Psychedelics such as psilocybin produce a tolerance, so you might see diminishing returns after a few days. This is why Fadiman suggests leaving a couple of days between each dose.

Additionally, the fact that positive effects can be felt sometimes many days after a microdose is a good reason to space out your doses.

Concern for your health is another reason to avoid microdosing every day. There is a potential heart risk of taking too many psychedelics over a long period of time. Although we don't know how this translates when it comes to microdosing, its probably best to err on the side of caution, and avoid microdosing too frequently, or for longer than a few months at a time.

Another downside to microdosing every day is normalizing a very potent substance. You can compare it to the use of coffee for productivity purposes. When you drink coffee every day, over time you need to increase the dose to get the same effect. Within a couple of months, one cup turns into two, three, or four cups.

It is best to leverage microdosing as an occasional advantage, rather than a consistent go-to like coffee.

MICRODOSING RETREATS

For people who are new to psychedelics, even microdosing can be a daunting concept. But retreats are an exciting option for those who want to be introduced to psychedelics surrounded by experts in a guided, personalized setting.

The Synthesis retreat in Amsterdam is curated by microdosing experts, and is designed to offer each participant a perfect introduction to psychedelics.

Curated microdosing retreats could be an option for people looking to begin their microdosing journey, and could be the best way to translate the psychedelic experience into lessons for living a better life.

For those struggling with depression, anxiety, PTSD, ADD/ADHD, mood disorders and/or addiction (to name a few), microdosing can create a number of positive changes.

Clinical research has shown that larger doses of psychedelics are effective at treating depression, anxiety, and addiction. Anecdotal evidence backs up the idea that a regular microdosing regimen can also have healing benefits for sufferers of various mental health conditions:

"Microdosing doesn't allow me to be anywhere else but in the present moment. This has helped me tremendously with my anxiety and depression. I am incapable of worrying about what's going to happen next week, tomorrow, or even five minutes from now. I can function without anxiety for the first time in years. I feel that my attention span is greater, I'm concentrating like never before. When I was suffering with pain I was given a lot of prescription pain pills and was quickly becoming addicted to them. Microdosing instantly helped me stop taking the several pills a day I was taking just so I could get out of bed, and I haven't touched them since."

HOW TO MICRODOSE

Instructions

The basic PF Tek method is pretty straightforward: Prepare your substrate of brown rice flour, vermiculite, and water, and divide it between sterile glass jars. Introduce spores and wait for the

mycelium to develop. This is the network of filaments that will underpin your mushroom growth. After 4-5 weeks, transfer your colonized substrates, or "cakes", to a fruiting chamber and wait for your mushrooms to grow.

NOTE: Always ensure good hygiene before starting: spray an air sanitizer, thoroughly disinfect your equipment and surfaces, take a shower, brush your teeth, wear clean clothes, etc. You don't need a lot of space, but your environment should be as sterile as possible. Opportunistic bacteria and molds can proliferate in conditions for cultivating shrooms, so it's crucial to minimize the risk.

STEP 1: PREPARATION

1) Prepare jars:

With the hammer and nail (which should be wiped with alcohol to disinfect) punch four holes down through each of the lids, evenly spaced around their circumferences.

2) Prepare substrate:

For each jar, thoroughly combine ⅔ cup vermiculite and ¼ cup water in the mixing bowl. Drain excess water using the disinfected strainer.

Add ¼ cup brown rice flour per half-pint jar to the bowl and combine with the moist vermiculite.

3) Fill jars:

Being careful not to pack too tightly, fill the jars to within a half-inch of the rims.

Sterilize this top half-inch with rubbing alcohol

Top off your jars with a layer of dry vermiculite to insulate the substrate from contaminants.

4) Steam sterilize:

Tightly screw on the lids and cover the jars with tin foil. Secure the edges of the foil around the sides of the jars to prevent water and condensation getting through the holes.

Place the small towel (or paper towels) into the large cooking pot and arrange the jars on top, ensuring they don't touch the base.

Add tap water to a level halfway up the sides of the jars and bring to a slow boil, ensuring the jars remain upright.

Place the tight-fitting lid on the pot and leave to steam for 75-90 minutes. If the pot runs dry, replenish with hot tap water.

NOTE: Some growers prefer to use a pressure cooker set for 60 minutes at 15 PSI.

5) Allow to cool:

After steaming, leave the foil-covered jars in the pot for several hours or overnight. They need to be at room temperature before the next step.

STEP 2: INOCULATION

1) Sanitize and prepare syringe:

Use a lighter to heat the length of your syringe's needle until it glows red hot. Allow it to cool and wipe it with alcohol, taking care not to touch it with your hands.

Pull back the plunger a little and shake the syringe to evenly distribute the magic mushroom spores.

NOTE: If your spore syringe and needle require assembly before use, be extremely careful to avoid contamination in the process. Sterilized latex gloves and a surgical mask can help, but the surest way is to assemble the syringe inside a disinfected still air or glove box.

2) Inject spores:

Remove the foil from the first of your jars and insert the syringe as far as it will go through one of the holes.

With the needle touching the side of the jar, inject approximately ¼ cc of the spore solution (or slightly less if using a 10 cc syringe across 12 jars).

Repeat for the other three holes, wiping the needle with alcohol between each.

Cover the holes with micropore tape and set the jar aside, leaving the foil off.

Repeat the inoculation process for the remaining jars, sterilizing your needle with the lighter and then alcohol between each.

STEP 3: COLONIZATION

1) Wait for the mycelium:

Place your inoculated jars somewhere clean and out of the way. Avoid direct sunlight and temperatures outside 70-80 °F (room temperature).

White, fluffy-looking mycelium should start to appear between seven and 14 days, spreading outward from the inoculation sites.

NOTE: Watch out for any signs of contamination, including strange colors and smells, and dispose of any suspect jars immediately. Do this outside in a secure bag without unscrewing the lids. If you're unsure about whether a jar is contaminated, always err on the side of caution—even if the substrate is otherwise healthily colonized—as some contaminants are deadly for humans.

2) Consolidate:

After three to four weeks, if all goes well, you should have at least six successfully colonized jars. Leave for another seven days to allow the mycelium to strengthen its hold on the substrate.

STEP 4: PREPARING THE GROW CHAMBER

1) Make a shot gun fruiting chamber:

Take your plastic storage container and drill ¼-inch holes roughly two inches apart all over the sides, base, and lid. To avoid cracking, drill your holes from the inside out into a block of wood.

Set the box over four stable objects, arranged at the corners to allow air to flow underneath. You may also want to cover the surface under the box to protect it from moisture leakage.

NOTE: The shot gun fruiting chamber is far from the best design, but it's quick and easy to build and does the job well for beginners. Later, you may want to try out alternatives.

2) Add perlite:

Place your perlite into a strainer and run it under the cold tap to soak.

Allow it to drain until there are no drips left, then spread it over the base of your grow chamber.

Repeat for a layer of perlite roughly 4-5 inches deep.

STEP 5: FRUITING

1) "Birth" the colonized substrates (or "cakes"):

Open your jars and remove the dry vermiculite layer from each, taking care not to damage your substrates, or "cakes", in the process.

Upend each jar and tap down onto a disinfected surface to release the cakes intact.

2) Dunk the cakes:

Rinse the cakes one at a time under a cold tap to remove any loose vermiculite, again taking care not to damage them.

Fill your cooking pot, or another large container, with tepid water and place your cakes inside. Submerge them just beneath the surface with another pot or similar heavy item.

Leave the pot at room temperature for up to 24 hours for the cakes to rehydrate.

3) Roll the cakes:

Remove the cakes from the water and place them on a disinfected surface.

Fill your mixing bowl with dry vermiculite.

Roll your cakes one by one to fully coat them in vermiculite. This will help to keep in the moisture.

4) Transfer to grow chamber:

Cut a tin foil square for each of your cakes, large enough for them to sit on without touching the perlite.

Space these evenly inside the grow chamber.

Place your cakes on top and gently mist the chamber with the spray bottle.

Fan with the lid before closing.

5) Optimize and monitor coniditions:

Mist the chamber around four times a day to keep the humidity up, taking care not to soak your cakes with water.

Fan with the lid up to six times a day, especially after misting, to increase airflow.

NOTE: Some growers use fluorescent lighting set on a 12-hour cycle, but indirect or ambient lighting during the day is fine. Mycelium only needs a little light to determine where the open air is and where to put forth mushrooms.

STEP 6: HARVESTING

1) Watch for fruits:

Your mushrooms, or fruits, will appear as tiny white bumps before sprouting into "pins." After 5-12 days, they'll be ready to harvest.

2) Pick your fruits:

When ready, cut your mushrooms close to the cake to remove. Don't wait for them to reach the end of their growth, as they'll begin to lose potency as they mature.

NOTE: The best time to harvest mushrooms is right before the veil breaks. At this stage, they'll have light, conical-shaped caps and covered gills.

WHAT NEXT?

STORAGE

Psilocybin mushrooms tend to go bad within a few weeks in the fridge. So if you plan to use them for microdosing or you just want to save them for later, you'll need to think about storage. The most effective method for long-term storage is drying. This should keep them potent for two to three years as long as they're kept in a cool, dark, dry place. If they're stored in the freezer, they'll pretty much last indefinitely.

The lo-fi way to dry your mushrooms is to leave them out on a sheet of paper for a few days, perhaps in front of a fan. The problem with this method is they won't get "cracker dry." That is, they won't snap when you try to bend them, which means they'll still retain some moisture. They may also significantly diminish in potency, depending on how long you leave them out. Using a dehydrator is by far the most efficient method, but those can be expensive. A good alternative is to use a dessicant as follows:

Air dry your mushrooms for 48 hours, ideally with a fan.

Place a layer of dessicant into the base of an airtight container. Readily available dessicants include silica gel kitty litter and anhydrous calcium chloride, which you can purchase from hardware stores.

Place a wire rack or similar set-up over the dessicant to keep your mushrooms from touching it.

Arrange your mushrooms on the rack, ensuring they're not too close together, and seal the container.

Wait for a few days, then test to see if they're cracker dry.

Transfer to storage bags (e.g. ZipLoc, vacuum sealed) and place in the freezer.

REUSING THE SUBSTRATE

After your first flush, the same cakes can be re-used up to three times. Simply dry them out for a few days and repeat Step 5.2 (dunking). But don't roll them in the vermiculite; just place them back in the grow chamber and mist and fan as before. When you start to see contaminants (usually around the third re-use), drench the cakes with the mister spray and dispose of them outside in a secure bag.

MAKING SPORE SYRINGES

Filling your own psilocybin spore syringes is about as self-sufficient as it gets.

First, you'll need to take a spore print from a mature mushroom, i.e. one that's been allowed to grow until its cap has opened out and the edges are upturned. You should also notice an accumulation of dark purple deposits around the base. These are the magic mushroom spores.

To collect them, remove the cap with a flame-sterilized scalpel and place it gills down on a sterile paper sheet. Cover with a disinfected glass or jar to protect it from the air and leave for 24 hours. Keep the resulting spore print out of light in an airtight plastic bag.

To load a spore syringe, scrape some of the spore print into a sterile glass of distilled water. You can find this at auto supply stores. Then fill your syringe (which should also be sterile) and empty it back into the glass several times to evenly distribute the spores. Fill it a final time and place it inside an airtight plastic bag. Leave at room temperature for a few days to allow the spores to hydrate. You can then keep the syringe in the fridge until you're ready to use it. It should last at least two months.

ADAPTATIONS AND ALTERNATIVES

Numerous modifications have been made to the PF Tek method, both to increase yield and to make things easier. Different species also tend to produce better with different substrates and conditions.

The main alternative to the basic PF Tek is the monotub method, which involves spawning to bulk on coir (coconut fiber extract), manure, straw, or some other fresh and nutritious substrate.

Eventually you may want to experiment with some of these other methods, but the PF Tek is a good introduction for now.

Made in the USA
Coppell, TX
23 November 2020